Editor

Lorin Klistoff, M.A.

Managing Editor

Karen Goldfluss, M.S. Ed.

Editor-in-Chief

Sharon Coan, M.S. Ed.

Cover Artist

Barb Lorseyedi

Art Director

CJae Froshay

Imaging

Alfred Lau

James Edward Grace

Product Manager

Phil Garcia

Publisher

Mary D. Smith, M.S. Ed.

Shapes & Sizes

Kindergarten

Authors

Teacher Created Resources Staff

Teacher Created Resources, Inc.

6421 Industry Way

Westminster, CA 92683

www.teachercreated.com

ISBN-0-7439-3307-9

©*2002 Teacher Created Resources, Inc.*

Reprinted, 2006

Made in U.S.A.

Table of Contents

35 Hiding Frog

1. Cut along the thick lines ▬▬▬.

2. Fold ❶ in half.

3. Fold ❷ downwards along the dotted lines ▪▪▪▪ and upwards along the dashed line ▬▪▬ . Paste it onto ❶ as shown on the right.

4. Fold ❸ upwards along the dashed line ▬▪▬ and paste it onto ❷.

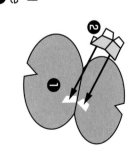

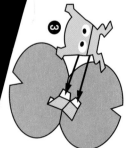

Introduction

The old adage, practice makes perfect, can really hold true for your child and his or her education. The more practice and exposure your child has with concepts being taught in school, the more success he or she is likely to find. For many parents, knowing how to help their children can be frustrating because the resources may not be readily available.

As a parent it is also difficult to know where to focus your efforts so that the extra practice your child receives at home supports what he or she is learning in school.

This book has been designed to help parents and teachers reinforce basic skills with their children. *Practice Makes Perfect* reviews basic math skills for children in kindergarten. The math focus is shapes and sizes. While it would be impossible to include in this book all concepts taught in kindergarten, the following basic objectives are reinforced through practice exercises. These objectives support math standards established on a district, state, or national level. (Refer to the Table of Contents for the specific objectives of each practice page.)

- Tracing shapes
- Recognizing shapes
- Identifying shapes
- Recognizing shape patterns
- Recognizing shapes and colors
- Identifying shape words

- Identifying shortest and longest
- Identifying smaller and smallest
- Identifying larger and largest
- Identifying smallest to largest
- Identifying biggest to smallest
- Identifying same size

There are 40 practice pages organized sequentially, so children can build their knowledge from more basic skills to higher-level math skills. Also, there is an answer key starting on page 44.

How to Make the Most of This Book

Here are some useful ideas for optimizing the practice pages in this book:

- Set aside a specific place in your home to work on the practice pages. Keep it neat and tidy with materials on hand.

- Set up a certain time of day to work on the practice pages. This will establish consistency. An alternative is to look for times in your day or week that are less hectic and conducive to practicing skills.

- Keep all practice sessions with your child positive and constructive. If the mood becomes tense, or you and your child are frustrated, set the book aside and look for another time to practice with your child. Forcing your child to perform will not help. Do not use this book as a punishment.

- Help with instructions if necessary. If your child is having difficulty understand what to do or how to get started, work the first problem through with him or her.

- Review the work your child has done. This serves as reinforcement and provides further practice.

- Allow your child to use whatever writing instruments he or she prefers. For example, colored pencils can add variety and pleasure to drill work.

- Pay attention to the areas in which your child has the most difficulty. Provide extra guidance and exercises in those areas. Allowing children to use drawings and manipulatives, such as coins, tiles, game markers, or flash cards, can help them grasp difficult concepts more easily.

- Look for ways to make real-life application to the skills being reinforced.

Practice 1

First, use your finger to trace the shapes. Then use a crayon.

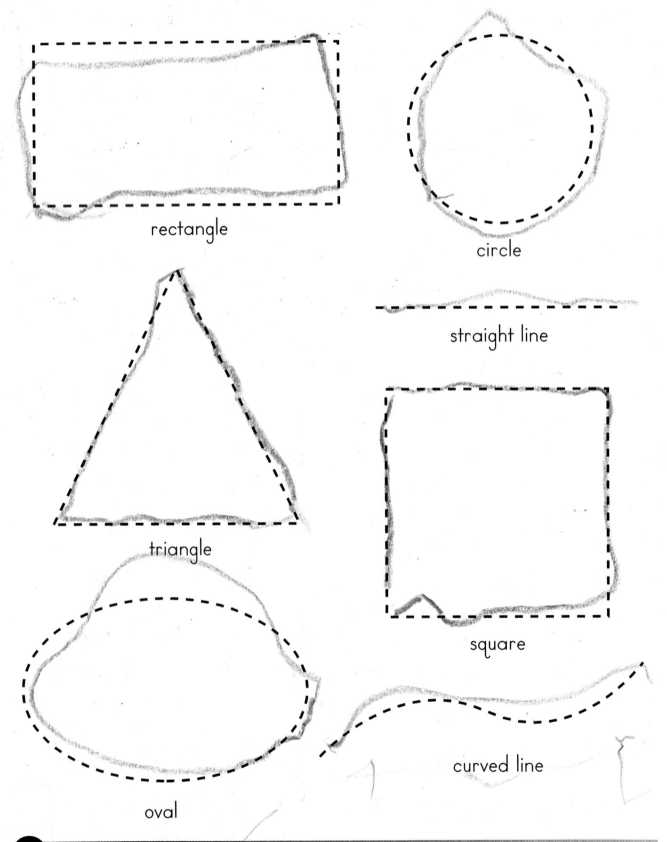

rectangle

circle

straight line

triangle

square

oval

curved line

Practice 2

Trace the shapes.

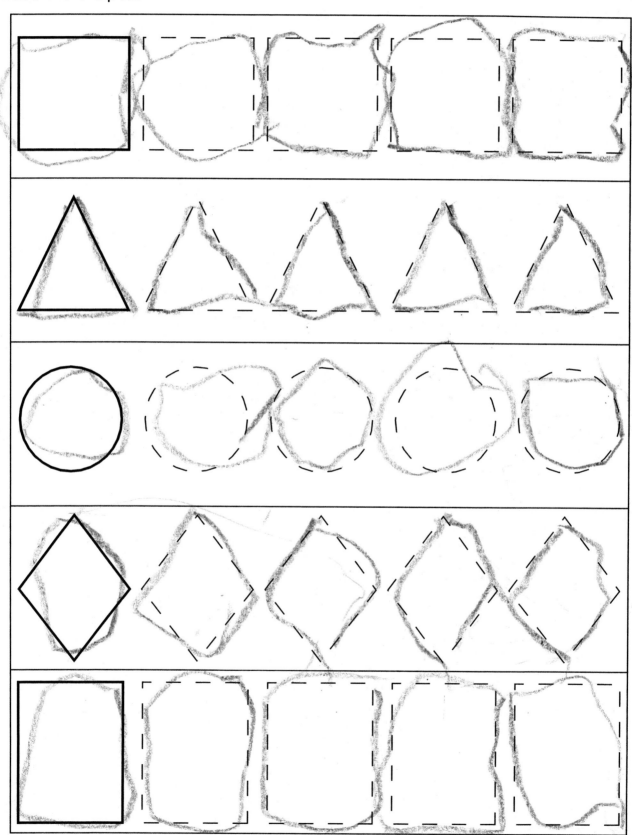

Practice 3

Trace each outlined shape with a finger, then trace it with a crayon. Name each shape and the instrument. Color the picture.

Practice 4

Color the circles pink.

Practice 5

Color the squares brown.

Practice 6

 Color the triangles orange.

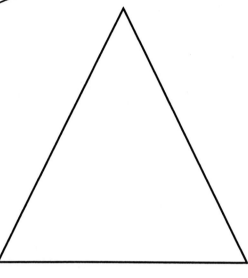

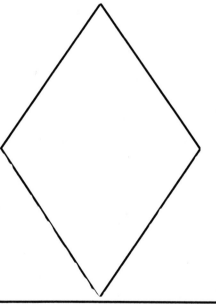
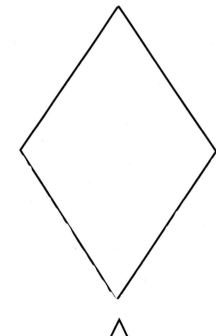

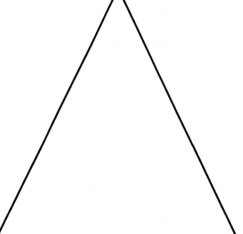

Practice 7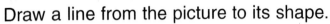

Draw a line from the picture to its shape.

Practice 8

Color the matching shape. Name each shape.

Practice 9

Draw a line from the question to the answer.

1. I have no points.
   I have no straight lines.
   I am round.
   What am I?

2. I have straight sides.
   I have three points.
   What am I?

3. I have four sides.
   I have four points.
   I look like a box.
   What am I?

4. I have rounded sides.
   When you see me,
   you think of love.
   What am I?

5. I have four sides.
   My sides are straight.
   I am not a square.
   What am I?

Practice 10

Draw a shape to finish the pattern.

Practice 11

Draw the next thing in each series.

1. 	
2. 	
3. 	
4. 	
5. 	

Practice 12

Color the △s yellow. Color the ☐s green. Color the ▭s red.

Practice 13

Color the ▭ s yellow.

Color the ⬭ s purple.

Color the ◇ s orange.

Practice 14

Find the hidden shapes in the picture of the clown.

Color all the circles red. Color all the squares green. Color all the triangles yellow.

Practice 15

Find and color these shapes: △, ▢, ○, ▭.

Practice 16

Color the rabbits brown. Color the rest of the picture.

Can you find ▢s, ◯s, and △s?

Practice 17

Color the ▢ s   blue.

Color the ◯ s   red.

Color the ♡ s   yellow.

Color the △ s   green.

Practice 18

Color the ◯s blue.

Color the △s green.

Color the ▢s red.

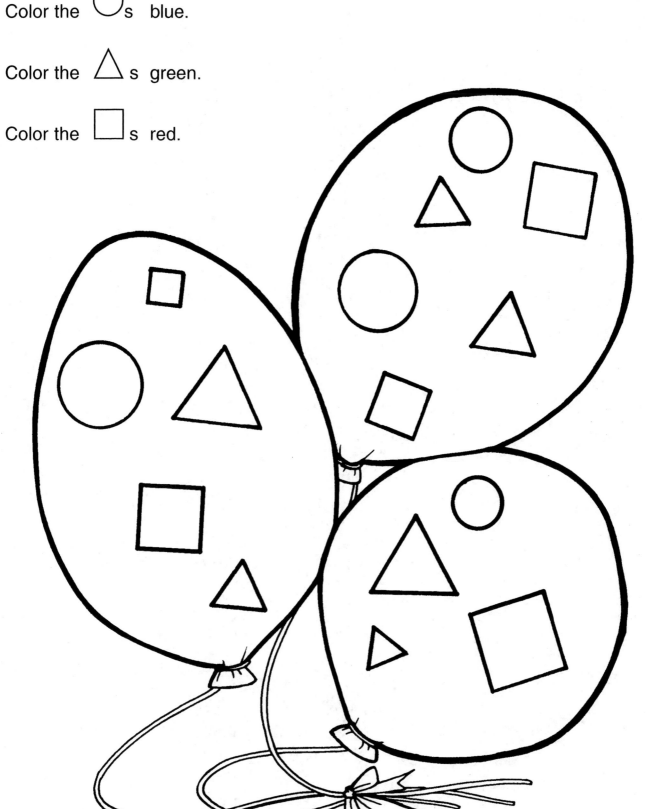

Practice 19

Color each shape at the top the correct color. Then color each shape on the picture to match.

Color all the following shapes:

△ red   ▭ green

○ yellow   ◇ blue

Practice 20

 Follow the shapes to color the picture.

■ = green   ▲ = black   ● = blue   ♥ = yellow

Practice 21

Follow the shapes to color the picture.

● = green   ■ = yellow   ▲ = brown   ◆ = white

Practice 22

Trace the name under each shape.

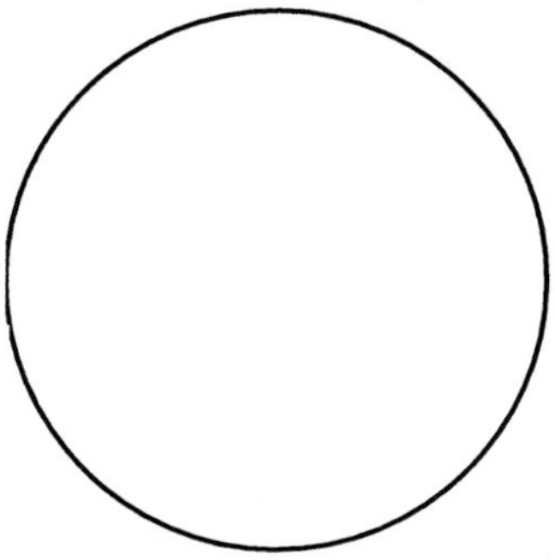

circle

square

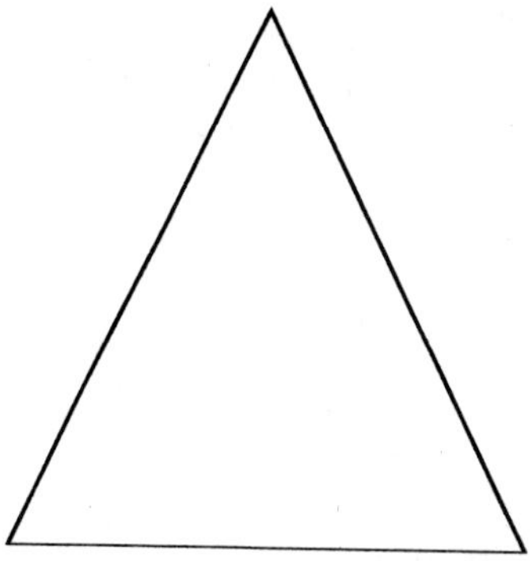

triangle

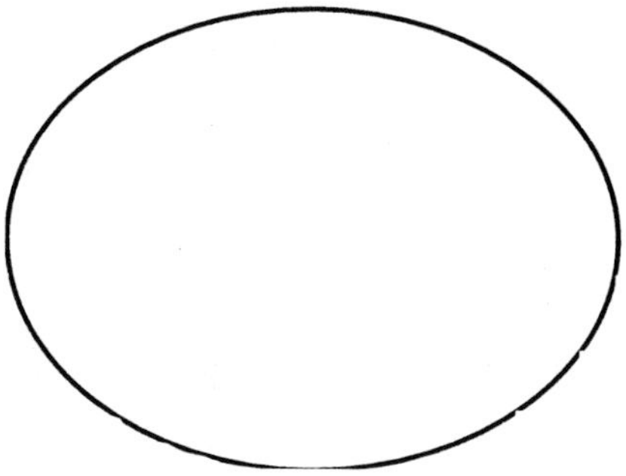

oval

star

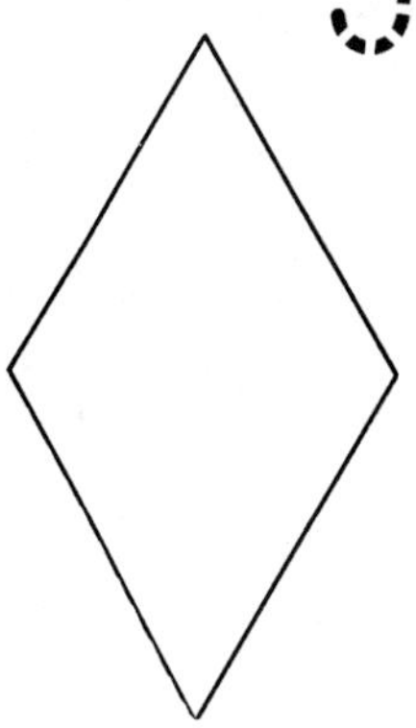

diamond

heart

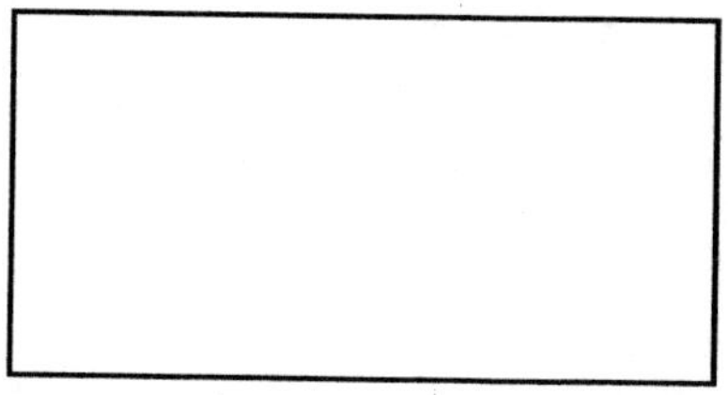

rectangle

Practice 23

 Draw a line to match each shape to its name. Color the shapes red.

heart

square

oval

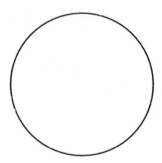

circle

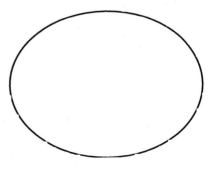

Practice 24

 Draw a line to match each shape to its name. Color the shapes green.

rectangle

diamond

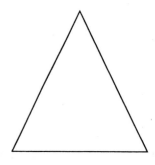

star

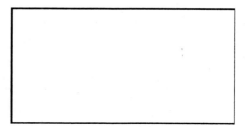

triangle

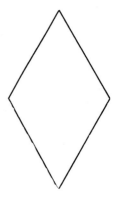

Practice 25

Draw a line to match each shape to its name. Color the shapes green.

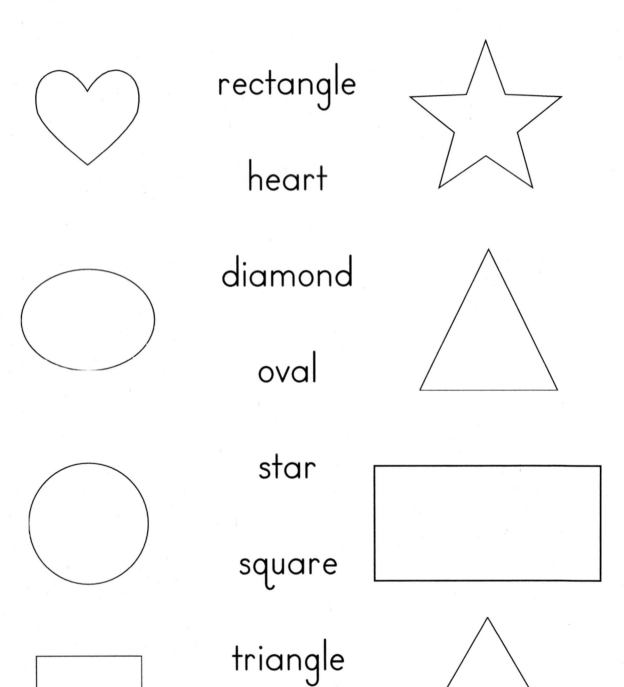

rectangle

heart

diamond

oval

star

square

triangle

circle

Practice 26

Write the name under each shape.

Practice 27

Directions: Color the shortest object in each row.

Practice 28

Directions: Color the longest object in each row.

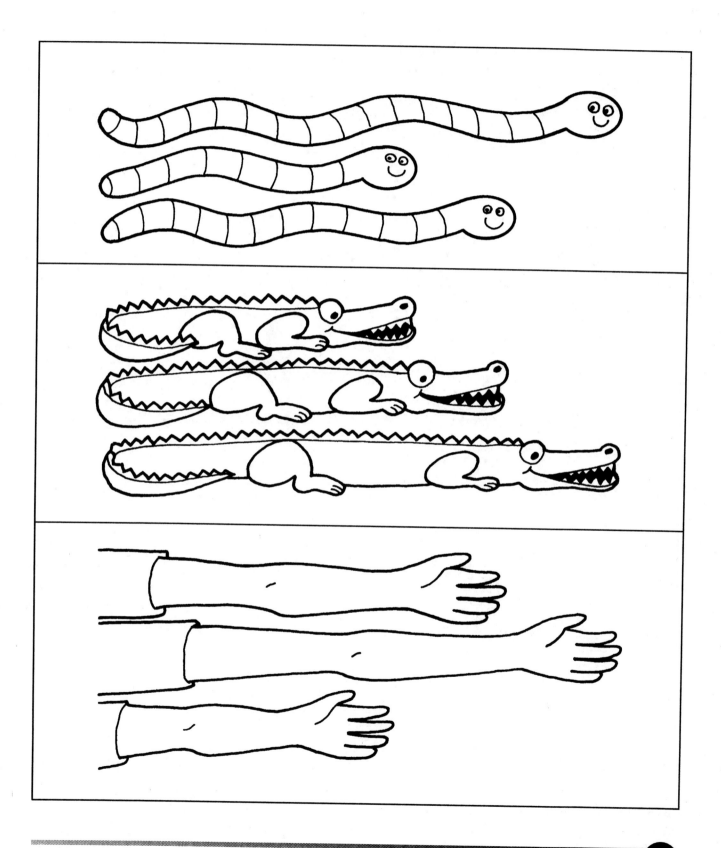

Practice 29

Color the smaller things in each box.

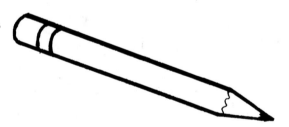

Draw three things smaller than the pencil.

Practice 30

Directions: Color the smallest object in each row.

Practice 31

Color the larger things in each box.

Draw three things larger than the pencil.

Practice 32

Directions: Color the largest object in each row.

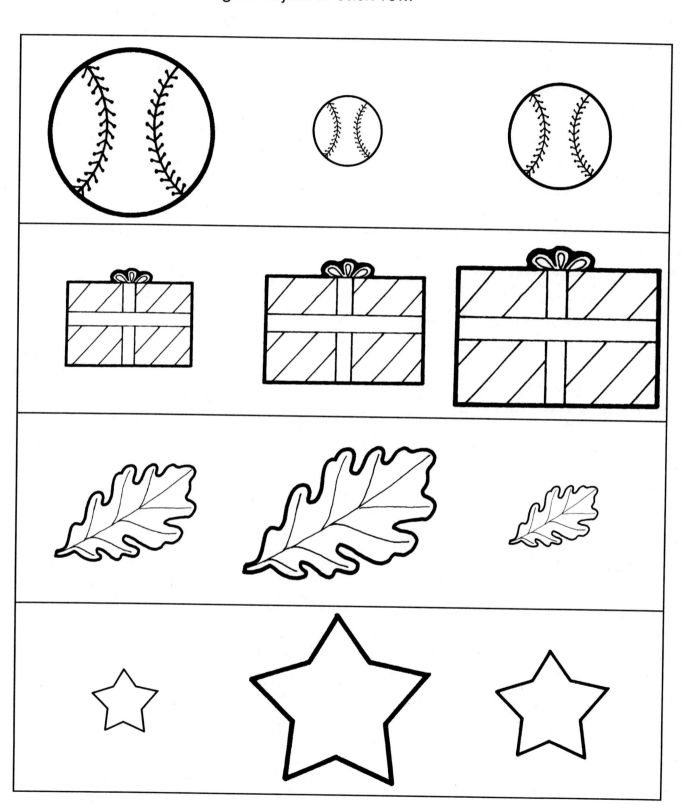

Practice 33

Match like big and small pictures. Color.

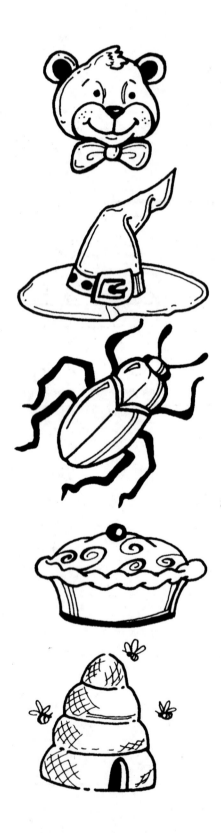

Practice 34

Color the big shoes blue.

Color the little shoes yellow.

Practice 35

Make a ● on the biggest shape in each row.

Draw an **X** on the smallest shape in each row.

Practice 36

Color the biggest things red.

Color the medium-sized things blue.

Color the smallest things yellow.

Practice 37

Write the number **1**, **2**, or **3** in the box next to each picture. Put the number **1** next to the smallest picture, **2** next to the medium picture, and the number **3** next to the largest picture.

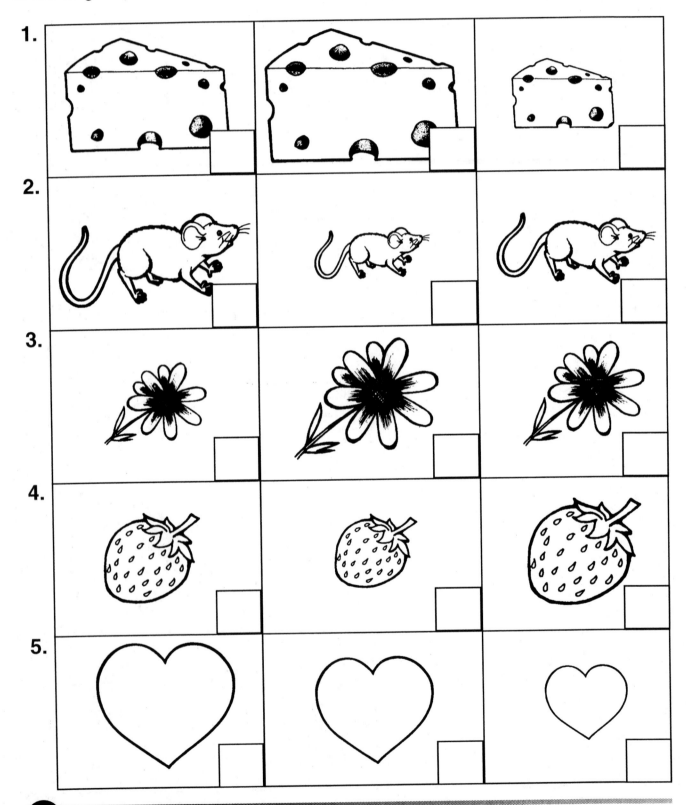

Practice 38

Color the lengths that are the same size.

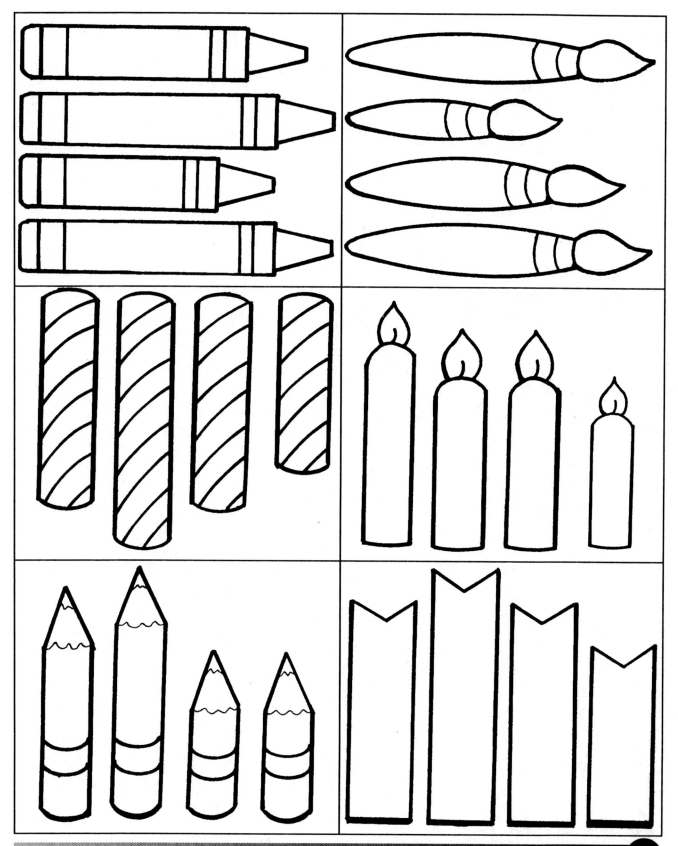

Practice 39

Draw a line to match the turkeys that are the same size.

Practice 40

Color the items that are the same size. Put an X on the item that is not the same size.

Answer Key

Page 4
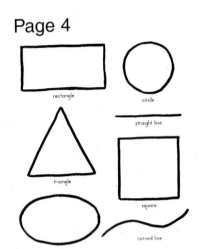

Page 5
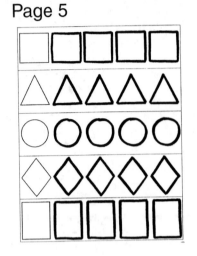

Page 6

circle / drum

circle / cymbals

triangle/triangle

Page 7
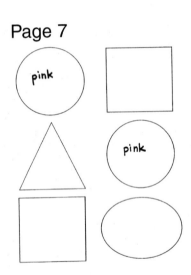

Page 8
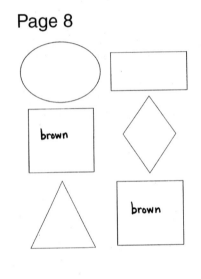

Page 9
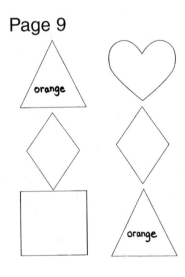

Page 10
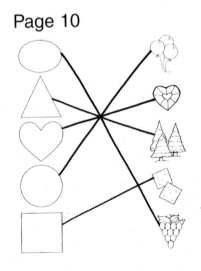

Page 11

Page 12
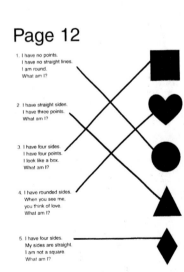

Answer Key

Page 13

Page 14

Page 15

Page 16

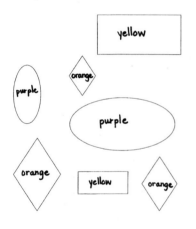

Page 17

Page 18

Page 19

Page 20

Page 21

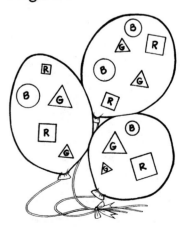

#3307 Practice Makes Perfect: Shapes & Sizes

Answer Key

Page 22

Page 23

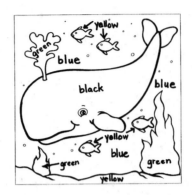

Page 24

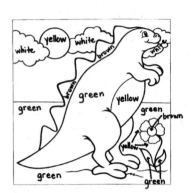

Page 25

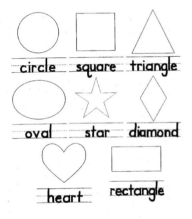

Page 26

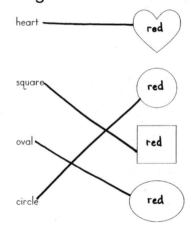

Page 27

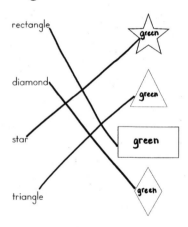

Page 28

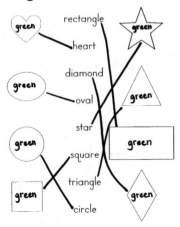

Page 29

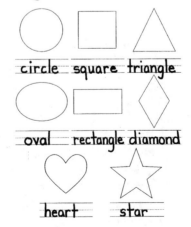

Page 30

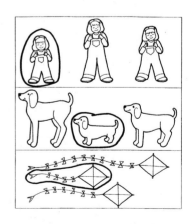

Answer Key

Page 31

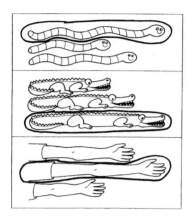

Page 32

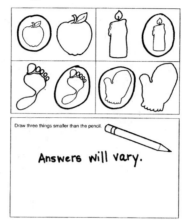

Draw three things smaller than the pencil.

Answers will vary.

Page 33

Page 34

Draw three things larger than the pencil.

Answers will vary.

Page 35

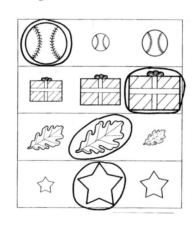

Page 36

Page 37

Page 38

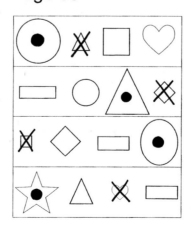

Page 39

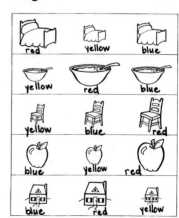

Answer Key

Page 40

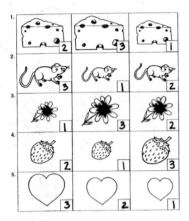

Page 41

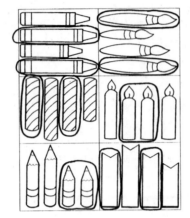

Page 42

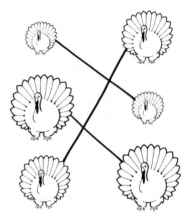

Page 43